SUPERMOM

By *Sandra V. Rozo, PhD*

Supermom: A No-Guilt Guide to Raising Happy Kids and Loving Your Life

Illustrations by Fernando Mayor, Daniel and Sarah Mayor-Rozo.

Copyright Ownership Declaration

ISBN: 979-8-9934655-1-7
Published by Sandra V. Rozo, 2025

Disclaimer

Supermom is a nonfiction work based on the author's personal experiences, reflections, and opinions. It is intended solely for informational and inspirational purposes and is not a substitute for professional advice, including but not limited to medical, psychological, financial, legal, or other personal matters. Readers are strongly encouraged to consult qualified professionals for guidance tailored to their specific circumstances. The views and opinions expressed in this book are those of the author alone and do not represent the views, positions, or endorsements of any institution, organization, or entity with which the author may be affiliated. This book is an independent work, separate from the author's professional roles and responsibilities as an economist. The author and publisher make no warranties, express or implied, regarding the accuracy, completeness, or applicability of the information contained herein. Neither the author nor the publisher shall be liable for any direct, indirect, incidental, consequential, or other damages arising from the use or application of the information in this book, including any actions taken by readers on the basis of its content.

To my ohana:
I love you with all my heart.

Acknowledgments

Our thoughts and ideas are the product of our life experiences and our interactions. This book is the result of my most memorable and impactful moments and deepest relationships. In these short words, I want to thank the special individuals who have helped me grow and become the author I am today.

First, I want to thank my gorgeous daughter for waking me up, for showing me the potential of the human mind and the immeasurable power of love. I am also incredibly grateful to Dani and Fer for supporting and loving me. The three of you (plus Vaca) are the engine of my existence and the reason I smile every day. I love you.

To my mom and my grandmother Tita, thank you for being such an inspiration. I want to be like you one day. To my dad, thank you for showing me the path to honesty and integrity. You are a remarkable human being. To my brothers, Nico and Juli, thank you for being such examples of courage. You are true gladiators. To my sisters of the heart, Cayis, Andreina, and Mari: thank you for listening to me. What a gift from life to have you all in my life.

Preface

Let me begin by telling you the story of my favorite supermom of all time, my own mother.

My mom was born in a small town of about 37,770 inhabitants called Mariquita, in the department of Tolima, Colombia. A character straight out of a Hispanic soap opera, she was the last of eight siblings, and as rare as it sounds, her family won the lottery right before she was born. The freaking lottery! Unbelievable, I know. I told you this story was going to be a soap opera!

After winning, her family became the wealthiest in town. My grandfather built the tallest building in Mariquita and opened a grocery store. Life—as my uncle describes it—was good. But then, when my mom was just eight months old, her father died of a heart attack. My grandmother went from stay-at-home mom to caregiver and business manager, all on her own.

I wish I could tell you things got easier, but as in any soap opera, a villain showed up. He tricked my grandmother into marrying him and stole all her money. Forced to start over, my family left their hometown and moved to the capital city, Bogotá. My aunt and uncle had to step up and help raise the family, and while my mom's childhood was filled with love, it was far from easy. She had to help financially from a young age.

My mom is an exceptional person. As a young woman, she worked full-time as a secretary during the day and went to college at night, funding her own education. She graduated with flying colors from a top business school and went on to become an incredible professional, a deeply loving wife, and a devoted mom of three. Although we had a beautiful family, her story did not have a fairy tale ending. As I was growing up, we faced truly difficult financial times. Still, through it all, she embodied what it means to be a supermom: working full-time, caring for us, loving my dad (another extraordinary human being), guiding us, and always giving her all.

When I think of my mom, I think of a truly brave and joyful soul, a courageous warrior mom. Through everything, she chose happiness. She shared her best energy with the world and always saw the good in others. She built a home filled with joy and gave her absolute best every single day.

Lately, I have been reflecting on her life, especially since she recently retired. Her generation became mothers during a particularly challenging time in history. Women entered the workforce full-time but were still expected to be full-time moms, as well: cooking dinner, grocery shopping, scheduling doctor visits, managing school prep, and running the household. Although things have improved and men today are more involved in chores at home, most of us women still carry the heavier load.

What my mom taught me is this: Even when life feels impossibly hard, we can pull it all off. We can do it all and still bring happiness and safety to our families. But sometimes, as we do so, our own well-being becomes the last priority.

I have lived that story. I have gone through the forgetting. But I also found my way back. Today, I live a more mindful and joyful life than I did just a few years ago. That's why I'm writing this book. I hope that by opening my heart to you, I can offer support and guidance on your own path. I hope that you enjoy this book as much as I enjoyed writing it. I hope that it helps you grow, learn, and rediscover your own joy.

Table of Contents

Introduction

I see you, supermoms of the world. Stay-at-home mothers, single mothers, working mothers, executive mothers, and business-owner mothers. I see every one of you. You are remarkable. You have hearts big enough to hold the world. They overflow with unlimited, unconditional love for your children and families. You are strong, brave, and selfless. You give your entire being without hesitation to bring joy to your loved ones, to protect them, to help them thrive. I see you because I am one of you. I am a multitasker-in-chief. I am a household chief executive officer. I am a friend. I am a woman. I am a professional.

I used to wake up every morning already overwhelmed. From the moment I opened my eyes, my day was packed: I was taking care of my children, keeping the household running, doing my best to be a competent and competitive professional, and somehow surviving as a human being. I moved through the day on autopilot, multitasking my way through my endless to-do list. Before I knew it, I'd be back in bed, exhausted and mystified at how another day had flown by. Then I would mentally list everything I did not get done, carry it over to the next day, and fall asleep.

And so it went. Days turned into months. Months into years. Time slipped through my fingers like sand. And I hardly noticed it happening.

I want to be clear: I was not miserable. I have always been a positive person. I still found moments to laugh and smile. But somewhere between the joy and the responsibilities of being a working mother, I had forgotten something important: I had forgotten to take care of myself. I had forgotten to live in the present.

It was not until the people who loved me most helped me wake up that I realized I was spiraling. Thankfully, I listened. I changed. It was not quick or easy, and many things happened along the way, but it became one of the most magnificent journeys of my life. A journey full of lessons, growth, and joy. A journey that changed me so profoundly that I felt compelled to share it with you. I feel a responsibility to help other mothers reach the other side of the shore.

That is why I wrote this book: because I want you to know that you can continue being the supermom you already are while also living a joyful and fulfilled life. You can shine your light on others without dimming your own. You can be present. You can be whole.

This book is a guide to help you on that journey. It is meant to remind you that your time on earth is precious and limited—that you too deserve a life filled with nurturing moments, dreams, laughter, and love. You can be a great mother *and* take good care of yourself. In fact, when you are happier, everyone around you benefits. Your energy radiates. Your joy becomes contagious.

This book is structured in three parts. Part One helps you lay the foundations of a joyful life. Part Two supports you in building the structure of that life with powerful habits and inner strength. Part Three invites you to design the finishing touches: defining your hopes, dreams, and goals.

Together, these pages are written with the objective of helping you transform every day into a colorful adventure full of meaning, love, and self-discovery. At the end of each chapter, I include a short summary with practical tools that you can use in your life—reminders of all the things we will learn together.

One last thing: In this book, I share with you my best knowledge about the most practical actions any mother can take to construct a truly beautiful and whole life. I also learned tremendously from writing it and must confess that I am by no means the perfect mother, simply a woman learning her way through motherhood. Hence, the advice in this book is also my aspirations for my best self.

Let's begin our journey.

PART I: SETTING THE PILLARS OF YOUR JOYFUL LIFE

Chapter 1: Feel Grateful for Your Motherly Transformation

I am the proud mother of two fantastic children: an eight-year-old boy and a five-year-old girl. Without a doubt, the most remarkable time in my life began when I became a mother nine years ago. Yet at the same time, this period has also been the most challenging. Memories of my life before I had children almost seem like those of a stranger, from another life entirely. The truth is that motherhood transforms us physically, mentally, spiritually, professionally, and socially.

In this chapter, I will share with you the most important changes that I have experienced since I became a mother. My goal is to inspire you to reflect on your own changes, learn to embrace them, and feel grateful for the woman they have made you today. I understand that we have become mothers through diverse journeys, so you might have experienced some of these changes (or maybe none at all). Some of you may have faced more difficult circumstances in becoming a mother than I did—or maybe your experience was a breeze! The differences aren't important. What matters is that, by reading this chapter, you realize that we all go through tough times, and we are all transformed in profound and unimaginable ways by motherhood. This chapter is an invitation to embrace your own changes and feel thankful for them. Being grateful is the first step on our journey to raising your energy and becoming joyful, empowered supermoms.

From Flat Belly to Full Heart

My first pregnancy brought me several physical surprises, even though I had previously been a healthy woman. The first, and most alarming, was a stroke in my right eye when I was three months pregnant. To this day, no one has offered any explanation for this event other than "You were pregnant, and anything that happens during pregnancy is normal." I still remember sitting in my office in the afternoon, working, when I began to see a black spot in my right eye. It was not intermittent; it was constant. That alone was concerning, but it was especially alarming to my husband, a stroke neurologist. At first, I thought it might be a migraine, so I called him. Until that moment, I had never heard fear in his voice when I complained about a medical issue. Normally, his responses were along the lines of "There, there. Take it easy. It's nothing! Take some ibuprofen; you'll be fine." This time, however, he fell completely silent. Then he said, "Call a cab, do not drive, and go to the emergency room now. I'll meet you there. Please, do it now." That response was terrifying. But I listened, and of course, he was right—it was serious. Thankfully, the stroke was small.

At the emergency room, I faced my first serious decision as a young mother-to-be when the doctors said, "We want to put you in a hyperbaric chamber to try to save your eye." I had no idea what that was, and my face must have shown it, because the doctor continued, "It's a high-pressure oxygen cabin. We have a short window to recover your eye before the cells die and you lose part of your vision. However, we've never done this with a pregnant woman. Although it should be low risk for the baby, the truth is, we're not certain. We've discussed your case with your obstetrician, and we all recommend that you do it. But I want to be clear, this is your decision. What would you like to do?" I decided a tiny black spot on one eye was not worth risking my baby, so I answered, "No, thank you, doctor. I won't risk my baby. The black spot isn't that big, anyway." Right then and there, I got my first physical souvenir from motherhood. Even now, nine years later, I still see that dark spot in my eye when I read. The good news is that my brain has adapted so I hardly notice it anymore. (Between you and me, I do think one of my eyes looks a little bigger than the other now. Hey, *c'est la vie*! At least I can read.)

After that, I got shingles on the upper inner part of my legs. Shingles is a painful rash caused by the reactivation of the varicella zoster virus, which I'd contracted when I was nine years old. It happened to me at exactly thirty-seven weeks of pregnancy. Shingles manifests as red spots that burn like fire on the skin. Not fun at all. And to finish my pregnancy off with a bow, I delivered my son by cesarean section, then undertook a brutal recovery, finding myself approximately forty pounds over my pre-pregnancy weight.

That was child number one. And by some sort of miracle, I forgot all about it, as many of us do, and got pregnant again two years later. My husband always jokes that childbirth can't possibly be more painful than a man's getting kicked in the private parts because, as he says, no man would ever ask for a second kick while many women choose to get pregnant again and again. The last time he said it, I rolled my eyes as usual, then I decided to seriously reflect on it, concluding that women forget pain more easily than men but have no trouble recalling adorable chubby cheeks and sweet, loving baby smiles.

Although my pregnancy with my daughter was smoother, I still had a twenty-seven-hour natural delivery and gained a lot of weight again. I really tried to eat healthy and exercise, but it turns out my body grows the most gigantic pregnant bellies I've ever seen (seriously!). Especially when I was expecting Sarah, strangers on the street would congratulate me for the supposed joy of carrying twins. (Please never comment on a pregnant woman's belly size!) Unsurprisingly, stretch marks crisscrossed my belly, even though I used every top-rated cream I could find. Additionally—to my embarrassment—I spent several months after Sarah was born terrified of laughing too hard, coughing, or sneezing, worried that I might pee my pants.

Following my pregnancies came the challenging months of breastfeeding. I know they are supposed to be these beautiful times, but in truth, for me, they were incredibly stressful, especially in the first weeks when I was a rookie mom. I constantly worried about producing enough milk and felt anxious about pumping to save breast milk for when I returned to work. I was convinced that giving my kid formula would mean failing as a mom—which obviously is not true! But even after trying every possible cookie, natural remedy, and trick the breastfeeding consultant recommended, I still developed mastitis multiple times with each child, and I felt overwhelming guilt for not always being able to give them what they needed. Of course, breastfeeding and all that intense pumping also changed my breasts.

After all that, I can tell you without hesitation that becoming a mother completely transformed me physically. Not in a way that makes me feel unattractive today, although in the beginning, that is exactly how I felt, but my body is simply different now. Over time, I have recovered somewhat and have worked truly hard at it. Still, the truth is that I am not the same, and with time I have accepted that.

Every woman is unique and our physical transformations are different—some harder, some smoother. Regardless of how hard or easy it is to recover physically from becoming a mother, as mothers, we should embrace and be proud of these changes. They are natural and should remind us that our bodies have done something extraordinary: They have created life. The visible changes should be reminders of that enormous miracle and of our forever-strong connection to our children.

This, of course, does not mean we stop caring for ourselves physically or we do not have healthy habits. It simply means we embrace who we have become and feel proud of the incredible miracle that our bodies are. Giving birth and breastfeeding are incredible miracles, but they are hard, and we should feel proud of the courage we show in going through them.

What is more incredible is that even after knowing how hard these moments are, and the transformation we had to go through, we would never change them, even if we could. We would never choose to go back, or even consider avoiding this experience, because now we have a ginormous life purpose, and our life is full of vibrant colors and adventures every day. So, let's embrace our new body. Our bodies are unique and beautiful, and we should absolutely feel proud of what we have experienced to get where we are.

My first request of you, dear reader, is that you reflect on your own physical transformation. Take five minutes and really remember everything that you went through physically to become a mother. Then look at your beautiful children and realize how much this experience has changed you, and how much it has helped you grow.

The Day the Wind Had Magic

For me, the spiritual changes occurred each time I heard my son's and daughter's first cries, although I have heard that for some women, this transformation happens at different times. I felt a monumental shift in my reality and my sense of self. I'm sure you understand what I'm saying: In that moment, I became fully aware that I was no longer the center of my universe. I was no longer my own priority. I also became certain that I would give everything to see my children happy and healthy. This shift brought with it an overwhelming sense of gratitude for the precious gift we had received in our children, and a promise to give my absolute best for them.

Our children also help us put the little nuances of life into perspective and rediscover many of its wonders (which we often take for granted) through their eyes and experiences. Sometimes, all it takes is their beautiful smiles to remind us how incredibly fortunate we are to have them in our lives and to let go of all the unnecessary dramas.

I will never forget one of these truly enchanting moments. During a trip to Argentina, I was chatting with my husband at the top of a mountain, when my son suddenly discovered the wind. Yes, you read that correctly: he discovered the wind. I wish you could see a video of him in that unforgettable moment: He closed his eyes, beaming, then opened his arms and shouted, "Mommy, Daddy, do you feel this?" And he began laughing out loud (*really* loud). We immediately joined him in rediscovering the incredible sensation we'd taken for granted for so many years: the feeling created by the magical wind.

I can imagine that you have also had your share of similar moments. Motherhood not only gives us a new and meaningful purpose in life but also allows us to rediscover the miracles of everyday life with fresh eyes. These are changes we should treasure and be thankful for.

Between Diapers and Deadlines

After my children were born, I became much more aware of the need to carefully balance my personal and professional life. I wanted to maintain a competitive career while also being a present and engaged parent. Since I became a mother, there have been many times—I wish I could say they were rare—when I have been plagued by guilt.

I am a working mother, one who is absolutely in love with her work, but despite this, I carried a persistent sense of guilt. When I was working, I felt I should be spending more time with my children. And when I was with my children, I felt I should be working those extra hours. At first, I thought it was just me. But even some of the stay-at-home mothers I admire most, who work around the clock caring for their families, have shared that they often feel guilty for taking even a few hours for themselves.

With time, I have come to understand that we need to be thankful for each of the different seasons and roles we experience in life and to stay fully present in each of them. We must become more conscious of how important these spaces are for our well-being. I invite you to do the same. When you are with your children, truly be there. Remember how fast life moves. Let go of distractions from the past and the future. Put away the cell phone and give yourself completely to the moment. Also try to be fully present when you are not with your children. It is important to have hopes and dreams and pursue them with purpose.

Every Stranger Is Someone's Child

The fundamental change that happens to many women after having children is that we become, in every way, better human beings. We care more about the planet and about treating others with kindness. Every stranger, in our eyes, becomes someone's child. In the spirit of supermom solidarity, we treat others the way we hope our own children will be treated.

Likewise, when we see a child struggling, our hearts break because we are reminded of our own children. This is one of the reasons I believe there would be fewer wars and conflicts if more mothers were involved in making those decisions. Few mothers would willingly harm another woman's child.

I used to believe that the main way I would leave a legacy in the world, some proof that I existed and contributed to making humanity better, would be through my professional work. However, over time, I have come to understand that our greatest legacy to humanity is our children: the traditions we teach them, the lessons we pass down, the values we share, and the way we love them will continue through them and eventually to our grandchildren. Through those traditions and values, we will live on for many generations.

This realization is what led me to start cooking. Before having children, I thought I disliked cooking, even though I'd never really tried. I also felt empowered as a professional woman when I said I'd never learn. When my kids were born, I realized that this mindset was a mistake for me (although I understand and respect that could be the right choice for others—different things work for different mothers).

I decided to change. From that moment in my life, delicious homemade food became my powerful love language. Over the past nine years, I have learned a great deal and have come to enjoy cooking. I hope my children feel loved through my food and that they will one day cook for their own families using my recipes. When they do, and remember me, even if I am no longer here, I will live on.

Having children has also made me more understanding of personality differences. My children have extremely different personalities, and they are both perfect in their own unique ways. One is incredibly extroverted and has a social superpower, making friends with ease. My beautiful daughter, in contrast, is slower to warm up to people. Her superpower is that everyone seems to love her instantly when she smiles at them. Through them, I have learned to be more patient in all areas of life, especially when interacting with other people. These days, I am more understanding when I come across colleagues who talk nonstop, as well as those who struggle to speak in public. I was not always like that—indeed, I was often impatient and, quite frankly, judgmental.

I would like you to take a moment and reflect on how being a mother has transformed you socially. Are you more understanding? Are you more patient? Do you care more for humanity and our planet? Be grateful for these changes: They ultimately mean you have become a better human being.

Embrace Your Transformation

After all the physical, mental, spiritual, professional, and social changes brought to us by motherhood, it is incredible that most of us would go through it all again without hesitation. I am sure many of you agree with me on this. When you have children, it feels as if your heart grows impossibly large, and you become capable of immeasurable and unconditional love. Your life becomes brighter, filled with color, and the little laughs and silly moments with your children become the source of indescribable happiness and the true reason for your existence.

What I hope you have realized by reading so far, is that motherhood transforms us in fundamental and truly magnificent ways. We should accept all these changes and see them as reminders of the journey we have experienced. These changes allow us to look into those beautiful eyes smiling back at us and to hear those sweet voices calling us "mommy." As mothers, we become stronger, wiser, more mature, empathetic, resilient, and compassionate human beings than we were before we had children. For those monumental reasons, we should feel grateful and embrace our transformation.

My next request to you is this: From now on, be consciously and intentionally grateful for becoming a mother, in whatever way that came about, and for the growth this experience has brought to your life: physically, spiritually, professionally, and socially. And yes, this includes stay-at-home mothers, who truly work around the clock, every single day.

It is a wonderful habit to begin your day with gratitude. Each morning, try to spend five minutes feeling thankful for being a mother and proud of the woman you have become. Gratitude is the first pillar of finding peace, raising your energy, and beginning the transformation of your life. You can express it in writing or simply reflect on it in your mind.

Here is a simple routine you can follow. When you wake up, immediately think of the most important things you are grateful for. I usually list ten, but feel free to choose the number that feels right for you. (This is your rodeo!) I always begin with gratitude for my family, my life, my health, my home, and the food on our table. Then I try to add different things each day that I am particularly grateful for. For example, today I felt thankful for my senses, the snow outside (it looked like a scene straight out of a movie), my job, my favorite aunt's birthday, and the miraculous gift of my eyesight. My senses, especially my eyesight, had a special place on my list today. I have high myopia, and every morning when I put on my glasses or contact lenses, I am reminded of the miracle of vision. The contrast between opening my eyes without glasses and putting them on is so vivid that, even now, at forty years old, I still marvel at how bright the colors become and how clearly I can see the details of trees and my children's smiling faces.

During your day, also try to be mindful about being thankful for the experiences that you have and for what you have become. You only have to say it in your mind. Everyday moments become more meaningful when you are consciously grateful for the privilege of experiencing them. Remember, life is made up of these moments, and by enjoying them, you are actually living a better life. Finally, at night, right before going to sleep, reflect on the day and try to identify one or two things for which you are thankful.

Practice these exercises every day. Be creative with them. Over time, you will discover just how much you have to be thankful for. This simple practice not only will help you recognize the abundance already in your life but also will attract even more reasons to feel grateful in the future.

Tools for Maintaining a Life Full of Gratitude

Gratitude is the first pillar of raising your energy and feeling better. The more you practice it, the more reasons you'll find to feel thankful. Use this simple daily guide to practice gratitude and bring more joy into your life.

1. Morning gratitude boost: As soon as you wake up, take five minutes to think about or write down five to ten things you are grateful for. Try to change them every day.

2. Midday pause: At least once during your day, take a moment to recall two or more items from your morning list. This short pause will help you refocus and bring awareness back to the good in your life.

3. Savor the simple moments: Find joy in everyday routines. A warm shower, clean water, healthy food, or a comforting cup of coffee. These small things are powerful reminders of how fortunate we are. Savor them. They make up most of our time, and they deserve to be celebrated.

4. End your day with a gratitude reflection: Before falling asleep, reflect on two or three moments from your day that brought you happiness or comfort. Reliving those experiences gently closes your day with a sense of peace and appreciation.

Chapter 2: Spoil Yourself with Unconditional Love

Over the past couple of years, my husband and I have faced some incredibly frightening medical tests involving our young daughter. These moments have been among the most emotionally challenging experiences of our lives. I am deeply grateful to say that our story has had a joyful outcome. During this time, however, while trying to be Supermom, create a happy environment for my family, keep up with my job, and manage our home, I almost always put myself at the end of every to-do list. In fact, to be honest, I don't think I even made it onto the lists at all. That time shook me to my core. Still, I somehow convinced myself that I was superhuman. I believed that I could carry all those emotions while juggling an extremely busy life, without ever expressing what I was feeling, allowing myself to feel it, or opening up to anyone.

I was completely wrong. Even though I had convinced myself that I was doing well, my body was not fooled. I began gaining weight, my face looked like that of someone much older than forty, and I started experiencing severe back pain. Eventually, I landed in the hospital with a diagnosis of appendicitis. You might think that was just a coincidence, but science shows a direct link between chronic stress and physical health. I am convinced the stress (and my choice to bottle up all my emotions) was directly linked to my hospital stay.

I wish I could tell you that after my hospital visit, I learned my lesson, went to therapy, or started taking better care of myself. But I didn't. It took many more months—and several brutally honest messages from my closest friends and family—for me to finally wake up.

The first message came from my husband. He is an incredible human being, and when he offers constructive advice, I know it comes from a place of love, so I take him seriously. A few months ago, we woke up one morning, and I smiled brightly at him. After smiling back, he gently touched my face and sweetly asked if I was taking care of my skin. He asked it in the kindest and most loving way you could imagine, just as you would hope someone who truly loves you would.

The second message came that same week from my mother, who was spending a few days with us. My mother is a wonderful person, and I believe that, as most mothers do, she sees my two younger brothers and me as the best thing that has ever happened to humanity, perhaps even the universe. She rarely criticizes us. Yet that day, she said to me, "Sweetie, it is important to also pamper and take care of yourself. I know it seems like there is no time, but there is always time. One day you will look back, and your health will not be the same."

The third message came that same week. (Yeesh, I must have looked terrible!) I went out to dinner with three of my closest friends, which, to be honest, was something I almost never did. But I love them, so I made the time. I was also relentlessly encouraged by my mother and husband to go out, enjoy myself, and have fun with my girlfriends. So I went, and I truly had a lovely evening.

In the middle of one of our conversations, my friends started talking about their nightly beauty routines. Trivial as it might seem, in that moment, I realized I'd not even *thought* about something like that, let alone *done* anything of the sort, for at least two years. I was always too exhausted to spend any time on my physical appearance (other than running, which I have never stopped doing), and I constantly had a million other things on my mind. But my friends were clearly doing a lot for themselves—for their skin, their health, their sleep, their nutrition, and their happiness. I stayed quiet, honestly in shock, because at that point, it was still very hard for me to open up and share everything I'd been going through.

The final message came a few weeks later from my beloved cousin—one of the purest souls I've ever met. Because she is so loving and completely free of judgment, she is one of the few people who can get me to talk about my feelings. For some reason, we had a few quiet minutes to talk, and I shared a little about what was going on, and to my utter horror, I burst into tears. She listened with love and patience, and at one point in our conversation, she said, "It would be good for you to talk to a therapist. I can recommend a good one."

After that conversation, the message finally came through loud and clear. The people who loved and cared for me could see that I was not taking care of myself. I might have been deceiving myself about this, but neither my body nor my loved ones were fooled. This was not something I did on purpose, or even something I realized, until all those people who loved me brought it to my attention. It was simply something that happened because I was on autopilot, so busy with a million things to do and constantly thinking of everyone and everything else except myself.

One thing that often happens to us when we become mothers is that we forget a simple truth: To care for others effectively, we must first love and take care of ourselves. We need to remember to love ourselves just as much as, if not more than, we love our families. Research shows a direct link between a mother's mental health and the mental health of her children. When we care for and love ourselves wholeheartedly, we are also caring for and loving our families in the same way. It turns out we transmit what we feel. If a mother is happy, her family is more likely to be happy, too.

Step One: Share and Write to Lighten the Load

In practice, beyond hugging ourselves, how do we give ourselves unconditional love? It begins with showing a deep sense of compassion toward ourselves, a compassion as genuine as what we would offer someone we love dearly. This naturally includes helping and caring for ourselves. In my case, it started with finding a healthy space to talk about my feelings.

You may not have intense emotions to unload like I did at the time—or maybe you do. Either way, it doesn't matter. All human beings need to express their feelings from time to time to feel better and live more peacefully. I recommend regularly talking to a therapist, a family member, or a kind-hearted friend. The only requirement is that you trust them and that they are good listeners. In my opinion, good listeners (especially those we trust) do not judge or try to fix things; they simply listen.

In my life, I have three wonderful listeners: my husband, my little brother (sixteen years younger than I am, a wise and beautiful old soul), and my cousin. I turned to them and shared everything I was feeling, over and over. What can I say? I had a lot of emotions bottled up inside me. I also began journaling, something I learned from my little brother. I absolutely love journaling and wholeheartedly recommend it. It has helped me reconnect with my truly joyful self, full of good energy.

How do you go about journaling? Simply write anything and everything that comes to your mind, without filtering, for a fixed amount of time each day. I write about my hopes and dreams, my life projects, my aspirations, my positive affirmations, and the things that worry me. I write what I would tell a friend, and even the things I would not tell anyone.

What I love most about journaling is that it allows you to express your feelings without fear and to pour your heart out. The paper is always there for you, offering a safe space with no judgment. Another thing I enjoy is going back and reading what I wrote. Sometimes I find thoughts that make me incredibly proud of myself. Other times, I see how much I have learned from my mistakes and how much I have grown.

In practice, it doesn't matter whether you choose to write or talk to someone, whether it is a professional or a trusted friend, or even do both. Any way of expressing your feelings will help you feel lighter and happier.

Step Two: Get Moving

The second step in my journey of self-love was taking care of myself both physically and mentally. I began to complement journaling with consistent exercise and meditation. I will talk more about meditation in the next chapter, so for now, I will focus on exercise.

Exercise is essential not only for your physical health but also for your mood, which in turn affects the mood of your entire family. It is time to stop making excuses. Just stop, please. This is one of the most important keys to a healthy life and lasting well-being. One helpful approach is to make your exercise time a nonnegotiable part of your day. You need your body to live well and to care for others. The healthier you are, the better a caregiver you will be. Make your health the top priority. Always schedule your exercise and protect that time.

Another helpful way to exercise more consistently is to break it into short, manageable sessions throughout the day. You could, for example, do two or three ten-minute mini-workouts. It is also important to find something you truly enjoy so that it becomes a sustainable habit. For example, if you enjoy talking with friends, you can coordinate with a neighbor and go for a walk together while you chat and catch up. You might also consider joining light meetings or talking to colleagues while you walk, if possible. Even tough discussions often feel easier and more productive while walking. Choose the stairs whenever you can. If you love nature, make time to go outside and move your body. One of the best investments you can make in yourself is to get moving every single day. Go on, begin today.

Step Three: Have Fun!

Another meaningful way to love ourselves is to have fun. Yes, you read correctly: fun. That familiar "me" time. When scheduling fun for everyone in our family, we rarely think about ourselves. Build a daily routine that includes a moment of joy for you, no matter how small. Even a short moment can help restore your energy and give you the chance to reconnect with nature, enjoy a hobby, or simply do something that makes you smile.

Do you even remember what it felt like to have a hobby? Someone recently asked me if I had a hobby or what I did for fun. I must admit, this innocent question took me by surprise. In fact, I had no answer at all and simply said, "Let me get back to you."

Do you have hobbies? What is fun for you? (Your answer should not include time with your children. Yes, I know exactly where your mind is going.) Think about what you truly love to do just for yourself and then go and do it. In my case, after giving it some thought, I remembered that I love gardening. I absolutely adore plants and flowers. Now, when the weather allows it, much of my "me" time is spent outside in the garden. I also love reading and writing. (What can I say? I'm a true nerd. But you probably already figured that out!)

Other enjoyable activities could include dressing up to feel beautiful, reading a good book, having dinner with friends, buying something lovely for yourself, styling your hair, or spending time in a cozy coffee shop. Dressing up and presenting your best self can lift your energy and boost your confidence. It is one of the many ways you can show yourself love.

Take some time to reflect on what fun means to you, and find a way to enjoy a little "me" time every day. If you have a husband or a partner, be sure to give them the gift of their own "me" time, as well. They too will blossom and smile more often.

So whatever makes your heart smile, do more of it. Life is too precious to save fun for "someday." Give yourself permission to have fun. The happier and more fulfilled you are, the more joy you will naturally share with those you love.

Tools for Maintaining a Life Full of Unconditional Self-Love

The second pillar in creating a joyful and fulfilling life is to love yourself deeply and without conditions. Simple, consistent daily actions can transform your energy and well-being.

1. **Unload your feelings regularly:** Make space to release what you carry. Whether it's journaling, speaking with a trusted friend, or talking to a therapist, choose the outlet that works best for you. Your mind and heart deserve room to breathe.

2. **Get moving:** Your body is your one and only home. Care for it. Exercise is not about pressure. It is about honoring your body and investing in yourself. Schedule it, protect that time fiercely, and show up for yourself every day.

3. **Have fun every day:** Make your joy a priority. Read, garden, dance, write, sing, or just rest. Do whatever brings you genuine pleasure. Fun is not a luxury; it is fuel for your soul.

Chapter 3: Strengthen your Spirit

I believe that although cultures and religions around the world use different names to refer to a higher power or universal intelligence, they often point to the same essential concept. Because of my upbringing and cultural background, I call this presence God. You might use a different name, shaped by your own life experiences and spiritual path. What matters most is not the specific word we choose, but the understanding that we are speaking about something profoundly meaningful, a guiding force beyond ourselves. As human beings, we should honor and respect the many ways people express their faith or spirituality.

Despite my coming from a deeply religious family, my faith in God recently went through a truly rocky period. To be honest, I am not entirely sure how I became so disconnected from it. I think it was partly due to witnessing so much chaos and suffering in the world, and to my own experiences. It was also influenced by learning more about history and becoming increasingly aware of how religion has sometimes been used in manipulative or harmful ways.

Rediscover the Light Within

A few months ago, while driving alone to pick up my parents at the airport, I reconnected with my spirituality. I had been going through a difficult couple of months, anxiously awaiting the results of a particularly troubling medical test for my daughter. That day was especially dark, and I was overwhelmed with fear. I often associate memories with colors that reflect the energy or mood of the moment, and this one feels gray. That grayness perfectly captures how I felt: I was not in a good place.

While driving, I decided to distract myself and started listening to the exceptional "Huberman Lab" podcast. This science-based show shares practical, evidence-backed tools for life. The episode that caught my attention that day featured an interview with Martha Beck, whom I'd never heard of before. Since that day, I've read all her books, and they have helped me grow tremendously and partly inspired me to write this book. In that episode, Martha shared her incredible life story about finding herself and her true purpose. It is a beautiful and moving testimony. I hope you get a chance to listen to it someday. As I listened to her recount her experience, I remembered something I had known earlier in my life but had somehow forgotten as I grew older: I was not alone. I had never been alone, and I would never be alone. God had my back, and we were going to be all right.

As I came to that realization, I was filled with the most beautiful energy. My chest felt as though it might burst with warmth and love. The emotion was powerful and overwhelming, but also incredibly beautiful. It was a special moment, one that I will always treasure and remember. That experience has fundamentally changed my mood, motivation, and overall happiness ever since. I will always be grateful to Martha and Andrew for recording such a deep, personal conversation and sharing it with the world.

Reconnecting with God and strengthening my spirit has played a central role in improving my emotional well-being and overall happiness. It has restored my self-confidence and filled me with a deep sense of peace. Most importantly, it reminds me to live with intention, to strive always to do good, and to be unapologetically myself.

As human beings, we have the extraordinary ability to restore and nurture our connection with God at any time. You have the power to choose faith and to strengthen it daily through prayer, meditation, or quiet reflection. You are one of God's greatest miracles. You accomplished one of the most amazing acts possible on this earth: As a mother, you created life. You nurtured and shaped another human being. Forget patents and gold medals: Your love and strength allow humanity to continue. If you're able to do that, then you can do anything. Absolutely anything. And if God gave you that gift, then faith is well within your reach. God is always with you. You are a miracle, and you are never alone. Remember this every day, and you will be well on your way to living a life filled with peace and joy.

Meditate or Pray Daily

There are many ways to strengthen our connection with God. For those who follow a specific religion, this connection may deepen through prayer. For others who define themselves as spiritual, it may be nurtured through meditation.

I begin each day with a prayer, right from my bed. My prayer always starts with gratitude for the many blessings in my life, just like the gratitude practice we explored in Chapter 1. Then I pray for my hopes and intentions for the day ahead. At night, my prayers complement my evening gratitude practice. After identifying two or three things I am thankful for from the day, I take a moment to reflect on how the day went, acknowledge any mistakes I may have made, and think about how I can grow from them or make amends.

A few years ago, I began meditating. I presume many of you are familiar with meditation, but just in case: Meditation is the practice of focusing your mind. It often involves tuning in to your physical sensations and grounding yourself in the present moment. For me, meditation is another powerful way to connect with the energy that created us all. Today, there is ample scientific evidence supporting meditation's benefits. It reduces stress, anxiety, and depression, improves chronic pain and cognitive function, and enhances emotional regulation.

To meditate, begin by focusing on your breath and what you feel through your senses. Gently guide your attention back whenever your mind starts to wander. This is often called "quieting the conscious mind." One way I connect with God through meditation is by visualizing His beautiful energy. I imagine it as a radiant, golden light, an immense ball of pure, positive energy. As I breathe in, I picture this golden light entering my body, and as I breathe out, I release all the dark, heavy energy within me. This practice helps me feel grounded, peaceful, and spiritually connected.

Another form of meditation I practice is spending quiet time in nature, focusing on the perfection and miraculous details of trees and plants. I choose to give my time and attention to plants because they fill me with joy and awe. Perhaps there is something in nature that you find particularly beautiful and inspiring, something that could help you connect with God as you reflect on its extraordinary perfection and complexity.

What I find especially helpful about meditating in nature is that it makes it easier for me to quiet my mind. I speak very fast—I once dated someone who confessed, many years later, that he could not understand anything I said when we first met, so he just laughed whenever I laughed. My friends and family would absolutely agree. But my thoughts move even faster than I speak. They constantly race from one idea to another without pause. Trust me, it is not always a good thing. That is why I call it my "monkey mind."

Because of my monkey mind, meditating was extremely difficult for me at first. However, little by little, I have improved, and I can feel the positive change in my mood every single day. Meditation is essential for personal growth.

If you practice it daily, you will begin to notice remarkable improvements in your quality of life. Start with just one minute after lunch and gradually increase the time until you reach a duration that feels right for you.

Thus, the third pillar in strengthening the foundation of your happiness is nurturing your faith or spirituality by creating space each day to meditate or pray. You need not spend a long time on this practice, but it does need to be consistent. This daily practice helps you find peace, manage stress, and become more open to the messages life is sending you—messages you might miss if you continue living on autopilot, jumping from one task to another on your endless to-do list. Make space for this sacred time, and watch how it transforms both your inner world and the way you experience life.

Tools for Maintaining and Renewing Your Spiritual and Mental Strength

Spiritual connection is the third pillar in creating a joyful, peaceful, and fulfilling life. Here are some simple daily actions to help you strengthen your spirit. Choose practices that feel meaningful to you, and commit to doing them consistently. Over time, these small steps build a deep, lasting sense of peace and spiritual clarity.

1. **Begin your day with gratitude and prayer:** Before getting out of bed, take a moment to say a short prayer. Start by giving thanks for your life, your health, your loved ones, and the gift of a new day. Then, set a clear intention for the kind of energy and actions you want to carry throughout your day.

2. **Use midday for a one-minute meditation:** After lunch, or during any quiet moment in your day, pause and breathe deeply. Visualize yourself breathing in golden, healing energy and releasing any stress or negativity. Even one minute can recharge your spirit and center your mind. Start with just one minute. Gradually increase your time until you reach five minutes.

3. **Spend time in nature:** At least once each week, find time to quietly observe nature. Focus on the beauty and detail of a tree, a flower, or the sky. Let that moment awaken a sense of awe and remind you of the perfection and love that surrounds you.

4. **End your day with reflection and prayer:** As part of your nighttime routine, after your gratitude practice, take a moment to reflect on your day. What went well? What could be improved? Is there something you could do to correct the mistakes you made? Offer a prayer of thanks and ask for strength and guidance for tomorrow.

PART II: BUILDING THE STRUCTURE OF YOUR JOYFUL LIFE

Chapter 4: Surround Yourself with a Loving Community

Let me share with you some of what we now scientifically know about the causes of happiness. A large portion of this research comes from one of the most fascinating and impressive studies ever conducted: the Harvard Study of Adult Development. The primary goal of this study was to understand the factors that contribute to a happy, healthy, and fulfilling life. Its key findings are summarized in the book *The Good Life: Lessons from the World's Longest Scientific Study of Happiness* by Robert Waldinger and Marc Schulz.

This study is the longest-running research project of its kind, having followed the same 724 individuals from their teenage years through old age for more than 80 years. It includes participants from two very different backgrounds: students and individuals from vulnerable neighborhoods in Boston. Today, researchers are also studying the lives of the more than 2,000 children of the original participants.

What makes this study so remarkable is that its conclusions are not based on participants' memories or reflections. Instead, the findings come from decades of ongoing, real-time data collection. To answer the study's central question, researchers gathered data—of nearly every kind you can imagine—over the decades: DNA samples, medical records, videotaped interviews, blood tests, hair samples to assess stress levels, and countless surveys. Astonishingly, the study finds that strong, meaningful relationships are the single most important determinant of living a joyful and fulfilling life. Let me say it again: Relationships are the number-one predictor of joy.

In other words, our social connections to family, friends, and community matter more for our happiness and health than wealth, fame, or career success. The study reveals that individuals with stronger social bonds are physically healthier and live longer than those with weaker connections. They are also more resilient to pain and enjoy better cognitive and physical health. Most importantly, the researchers discovered that it is not the *number* of relationships that matters most but the *quality* of those connections.

Invest in Genuine Friendships

One of the most powerful ways to transform into our happiest, most fulfilled selves is to surround ourselves with a close, strong, and loving community of friends and family. Naturally, this requires a significant investment of time and effort. Relationships grow when we give others our time and attention. This can be especially challenging for mothers, who often have little time to spare. Even so, it is essential to carve out time and space for connection. Think of the time you spend nurturing your relationships as one of the most valuable investments in your happiness, well-being, and overall quality of life. Consider it your social capital, the backbone of a joyful life.

Although I love technology and deeply appreciate the many incredible ways it has improved our lives, I also believe it has made it easier to feel lonely. It can lead us to immerse ourselves in social media without truly connecting with another human being in a meaningful way. We often spend time scrolling and can hardly remember what we read even the next day. We must instead make a conscious decision to build and invest in time with a community of friends and family away from mobile phones and computer screens.

Even as an extrovert, over the last ten to fifteen years, I became deeply immersed in my professional career while trying to be the best mother I could possibly be. Along the way, as life turned its wheels, I grew somewhat distant from old friends back home and formed only a handful of close connections during my graduate program. As time went on and these friends and I graduated, most of us relocated to different cities. Although we maintained a friendly bond, geographical distance gradually created emotional space between us. Then, as an incredible gift from life, when we moved from Los Angeles to Washington, D.C., where I now live, I was fortunate to meet a wonderful new group of friends.

I met my girls while waiting outside of my son's new tennis class. We met at slightly different times, and little by little, we began seeing each other more often, until we became close. I instantly connected with the three of them because of their authenticity and incredible energy. They are transparent and uplifting—seemingly completely incapable of giving off even an ounce of bad energy. Exactly the kind of friends I love to have.

They have changed my life, and I feel happier because of them. Let me tell you why: There are certain things only another mother can understand. Some feelings are so specific to motherhood that only another mom can fully relate. Having a group of close friends with whom I can just be myself, free from judgment, and laugh at our shared mistakes and common experiences is priceless.

My girlfriends have become part of my family and have taught me countless lessons and tricks on how to be a happier supermom. One of the most powerful things they have done for me is help me realize that I needed to take better care of myself. They never had to say, "You look exhausted" or "You need a break." Instead, simply hearing them talk about their own routines and self-care made me see how much I was neglecting my own well-being. We learn best through example, and I have learned a lot just from observing and hearing how my friends prioritize themselves.

Surround yourself with genuine friends who radiate positive energy and make you feel good about yourself. Remember: You do not have to be friends with everyone. All you need is a small group of close, genuine friends. They can make an extraordinary difference in your life. Also make the effort to visit and reconnect with those special friends who live far away and cherished ones who live nearby. Just like plants, friendships need to be watered and nurtured. Invest in your relationships by being generous with your time. Listen deeply, be supportive, and open your heart. All the love you give will come back to you many times over again.

One of the most important lessons I have learned in life is that when you give, you receive. Your recompense may not always come from the same person, but it always finds its way back to you. So be generous with your community. Go beyond yourself; be kind, thoughtful, and present. In return, you will experience extraordinary gifts that often seem to appear out of nowhere.

Invest Time in Your Family

While friends are incredibly important, the core of your social connections is your family, the family you grew up with, and the one you have created as an adult. I feel incredibly fortunate to be very close to my parents and siblings. I always make a conscious effort to be present in their lives and see them as often as I can. Since we live in different countries, it is not always easy, but we always find ways to make it happen.

Be patient with your family, and love them with all your heart. The time you spend with them is likely to be limited, so treasure it as a magnificent gift. Invest in quality time with your family and nurture that connection. If you have grown distant from them, remember that it is never too late to reconnect. Life is short. Don't waste it on petty arguments or grudges that, in the end, hurt only you. Reach out with love, and do your part to keep your family bonds strong and warm.

Some of the family members you grew up with may no longer be here. Nonetheless, you can honor them by remembering the beautiful moments you shared and by telling your children about them. In this way, they remain part of your life and, in a powerful way, continue to be present in your children's lives, as well.

Most importantly, put your best effort and focus into maintaining a loving, peaceful environment within the family you have formed as an adult. Creating a positive atmosphere and fostering healthy relationships with the people you live with may be the most important key to happiness since these are the human connections that occupy most of your time and hold the greatest meaning. Remember that your children learn primarily through your example. They are always observing you, picking up subtle cues about how to treat others and navigate life.

By modeling healthy relationships within your own home, you are not only building a more joyful life for yourself but also laying a powerful foundation for the families your children will one day create. This is easier to achieve when you maintain a mindset of positive thoughts and energy. Emotions are contagious. By keeping a balanced mental state, you contribute immensely to a peaceful and happy household.

Finally, be patient. We all make mistakes, and many arguments are so minor that they will be forgotten within an hour. Choose your battles wisely. Keep the number of conflicts small, and let go of the ones that serve no meaningful purpose. Time with family is never wasted; it is the heartbeat of a joyful life.

Tools for Surrounding Yourself with a Loving Community

Your social capital is one of the strongest predictors of your overall happiness. Here are a few intentional actions you can take every day to nurture and strengthen a loving, supportive community of genuine friends and close family members:

1. **Nurture and strengthen your genuine friendships**: You do not need a large circle of friends, just a few truly meaningful relationships. Deep friendships require time, energy, and care. Be generous with your attention and affection. Make time to reconnect with good old friends as well. The bonds you have built over a lifetime are incredibly valuable and worth sustaining. Go out of your way to visit, call, or write to those dear to you, and let them know how much they still matter to you.

2. **Build and maintain strong family relationships:** Make a consistent effort to stay connected with the family you grew up with. Spend time with them when possible, and nurture those relationships with love and presence. Most importantly, invest deeply in the family you have created as an adult. Give your best to keep your home environment healthy, joyful, and strong. Your family relationships will have the greatest impact on your well-being and serve as the model your children will carry into their own future families. Remember that

long after the details of daily life fade, the love and care you pour into your family will remain, shaping their memories, strengthening their values, and becoming part of your legacy.

Chapter 5: Create the Habit of Producing Positive Thoughts

The second step in building a solid foundation for transforming yourself into a joyful supermom is to develop the habit of generating positive thoughts. I often picture our minds as highways and our thoughts as different kinds of automobiles. Any car, regardless of color, size, model, or year, can drive onto a highway, just as any thought can enter our minds. Some thoughts are incredibly useful and empowering, while many others, perhaps even the majority, are not. Most thoughts are old, broken-down cars with damaged exhaust pipes that cause others to cough and create traffic jams. Although we cannot prevent every thought from entering, we do have the power to train our minds to redirect our attention toward more helpful and productive thoughts—to restrict which cars are allowed onto our mental highway. Only clean, reliable, high-performing vehicles get a pass.

The most incredible power we have as human beings, what truly sets us apart from other living things on this planet, is our capacity to have thoughts. This power is not only limited to producing thoughts; it also extends to the ability to be meta-thinkers. We can think about our thoughts. We can analyze them and reflect on them. No other living beings on Earth can reflect on their thought processes. This is an extremely powerful ability, one that can boost our well-being and success in life but can also lead to self-destruction.

The quality of our thoughts determines the quality of our emotions, our success, and most importantly, our level of joy and energy. You can decide to fill your mind with positive thoughts most of the time.

Remember: You are the master of your mind, not the other way around. You can choose which thoughts to focus on and which ones to discard. Only you decide which thoughts deserve a place in your mind. Be selective and disciplined because when you choose your thoughts, you are choosing between a virtuous cycle or one of destruction in your life. The more positive thoughts you allow, the more happiness and prosperity you will experience. The opposite is also true. Negative thoughts are like poison; they quietly erode your peace of mind and gradually wear you down.

People are not born with either a positive or a negative mindset. A positive mindset is a habit that can be developed at any point in our lives. With commitment and consistent practice, it is within reach for anyone, regardless of age, circumstance, or timing. Below, I share a list of the practices and exercises that I have found most helpful for maintaining a positive state of mind.

Step One: Spin Thoughts Toward their Positive Forms

The first step is to begin paying attention to where your mind wanders. Whenever you recognize a negative thought (which everyone experiences often throughout the day), immediately redirect your attention to something positive. How can you do this? Try to spin that same thought into something more uplifting. There is almost always a way to reframe a situation in a more positive light. For example, if you made a mistake, replace "I am so stupid" with "I will learn from this, and it won't happen again, or at least not as often." You can always view mistakes as opportunities to grow and failures as lessons on what not to do the next time.

Sometimes, however, you may notice thoughts that are so negative or repetitive that they are simply not helpful. These thoughts do not deserve space in your mind. For those, I imagine what I call the "trash can of useless thoughts." I picture a giant silver trash can in my mind that magically appears whenever I identify a thought that no longer serves me. It opens, absorbs the thought, pulverizes it, and disappears. For example, reliving past experiences that caused pain, questioning why they happened, and wondering why life feels unfair are exactly the types of thoughts I mentally dispatch into the pulverizer.

The more you recognize and actively replace negative thoughts, the easier it becomes to reduce their frequency.

Your mind will learn over time to produce fewer negative thoughts and more positive ones. It is a momentum-building process. With discipline and persistence, staying positive becomes second nature. You'll find yourself doing it almost automatically.

Remember that building this habit takes time and self-awareness. If you catch your mind spiraling into negativity, don't feel discouraged. Instead, pause, recognize the negative thought, and replace it right away.

The more positive you are, the better outcomes you attract in life. It makes sense: When you radiate positivity, people enjoy being around you. Think about the people you love spending time with. Most likely, they have a certain light about them. They are sincere and unpretentious, tending to see the world from a hopeful perspective. Rarely do we seek out people who are constantly pessimistic or who talk only about what is going wrong. Of course, it's okay to be down sometimes (we all are), but persistently negative people are not energizing to be around.

Positivity does more than make you likable. It helps you welcome new opportunities, take on challenges, and believe in your own abilities. You naturally move forward with hope, which often leads to growth and achievement. Being positive builds your self-confidence and is one of the most powerful strategies you can use to live a joyful and successful life. In fact, the more positive you are, the more luck you will seem to have. But my dear supermom friends, it is not luck at all: It is the power of your thoughts shaping your reality.

Positivity also means choosing to think positively about others. Do not trash talk, even if unkind thoughts enter your mind. Choose not to give them space. Everyone has both strengths and weaknesses, but you can always focus on the positive side of people. I want to emphasize that this is a choice you can make at any time. That does not mean being naive or ignoring harmful behavior, but it does mean striving to look for good in people and situations as your default approach.

Positivity also means helping others whenever you can and doing your best never to harm or hurt anyone intentionally. I firmly believe that the more positive energy you give yourself and others, the more positive energy will be returned to you—not always from the same person, but it will come back.

Step Two: Work on Your Positive Affirmations

The second step is to work on positive affirmations about yourself. These affirmations are also known as autosuggestions—three to five thoughts about yourself that are kind, caring, and loving. Repeat these affirmations anytime you catch your mind berating you.

They might sound like this: "I am beautiful, intelligent, happy, funny, strong, loved, successful, sexy, and money comes easily to me. I am also an extraordinary mother and woman and the best guide for my children. I am proud of all that I accomplish and the support I give to my family every day."

If these exact words do not work for you, come up with your own and memorize them. If you repeat these affirmations enough times, your subconscious mind will start believing them, and you will begin to embody them.

What is the subconscious mind? Your subconscious operates below your conscious awareness—the autopilot part of your mind that oversees automatic processes such as breathing, digestion, driving, your menstrual cycles, and your instinctive reactions based on past experiences. It is also where your beliefs, habits and emotions are stored, influencing your thoughts and behaviors when you're not aware.

If you repeat something enough times and with enough frequency, your subconscious mind will record it, believe it, and accept it as truth. It is the same process that occurs when you perform an activity many times, such as driving or returning to your house every day. After so many repetitions, you do not even need to consciously think about where you are going because your subconscious mind will take you there. In the same way that you let your subconscious mind drive or guide you home on autopilot, you can also train it to be positive and develop extremely high self-confidence. One day you will not need to try; your positive autopilot will take charge.

In short, always be conscious of the way you speak about yourself and the perspective you decide to take in every situation you face in life. You are training your subconscious mind when you make these choices. Be aware that it can also be trained to be negative if that becomes your default.

Step Three: Closing the Door on Negativity

The third step is to try to keep a healthy distance from individuals who produce a lot of negative thoughts. Negativity can be contagious! It is often difficult to completely isolate ourselves from individuals who choose to be negative because often they are our colleagues, friends, or family members. In that case, actively work to protect your thoughts. This can be done by cutting conversations short, changing topics, and talking with them about something they enjoy, something that keeps them away from negative comments and energy.

Everyone has something that makes them shine, so try to find out what it is and talk to those individuals about the things that turn their lights on. I have learned that often people become extremely positive when you talk to them about their children or grandchildren; this could be a strategy worth trying. Avoid, at all costs, indulging with negative folks in topics that make them emanate their negative energy toward you. Energy is easily transmitted, and so you benefit the most when you surround yourself with positive individuals who lift you up rather than bring you down.

Finally (this is important!), try to limit the social media that you use during the day. Why spend so much time of your day looking at a screen if we can enjoy the miracles of nature and life? Extensive research documents the negative mental health consequences of social media in not only children but also adults, so make a conscious effort to limit it. Not only is it harmful to you; it also sets a poor example for your children. In fact, recent studies suggest that children feel sad and frustrated when their parents are constantly staring at screens. Of course, we all want to stay informed, especially in today's world. Just set a timer, get what you need, and then stop. Just stop.

Please do not spend your precious "me" time on your phone; life is too short, and reality is far too miraculous to waste it that way. Because I realized I was truly addicted to some social media apps, I no longer have them on my phone and only check them for a few limited minutes on my computer. My intention in removing them was to be informed of what is happening in the world and with the people in my network, but to do so with clear boundaries instead of throughout all my waking hours.

The one message I want you to remember is this: You have the power to shape your life in any way you desire by using your thoughts and building the habit of being a positive supermom. The one thing you can fully control in life is your mindset. The more you choose positive thoughts, the more joyful, meaningful, and fulfilling your life will become.

And never forget that your children are watching. With every word you say and every choice you make, you show them how to face life. By living with a positive mindset, you give them an invaluable gift: the example of resilience, hope, and joy. If you do nothing else, let that be your legacy. It will make a lasting difference in their lives.

Tools for Creating the Habit of Producing Positive Thoughts

Commit to positive thinking to build a joyful mind and model these behaviors for your children. Below are actions you can practice every day to create the habit of producing positive thoughts:

1. **Reframe negative thoughts immediately:** Whenever a negative thought enters your mind, pause and consciously redirect it into something more positive or empowering. Treat each challenge as an opportunity to grow rather than a setback.

2. **Repeat positive affirmations out loud:** Each day, say three to five positive affirmations about yourself. Say them with belief and emotion, especially when you catch yourself being self-critical.

3. **Visualize the "trash can of useless thoughts":** Imagine discarding unhelpful, repetitive, or harmful thoughts into a mental trash can. See them disappear: being absorbed, destroyed, and cleared from your mind.

4. **Limit social media to protect mental space:** Set clear time limits on social media use and avoid scrolling during "me" time. Instead, use those moments to reflect, meditate, or enjoy the beauty around you.

5. **Surround yourself with positive influences:** Be mindful of the energy people bring

into your life. Spend time with those who lift you up and, when necessary, gently steer negative conversations to more uplifting topics.

6. Teach positivity through example: Be intentional about how you express yourself around your children. Choose kind, encouraging words about yourself and others, especially when discussing mistakes or frustrations. Your attitude becomes their model for how to face life.

Chapter 6: Become Your Inner Warrior

Human life is full of joy and fabulous moments but also, inevitably, difficult times. When we face these situations, it is extremely important to face them with courage, learn from our experiences, and move on, letting go of the negative emotions they leave behind. Constantly reliving bad, frustrating, or sad situations and their associated feelings is extremely unproductive and painful. Nothing good comes out of repetitive negative thoughts. In the same way that positive thoughts attract good things, negative thoughts can also bring chaos into your life. Because we tend to have repetitive thoughts day after day, if we choose to obsess about something negative, we will constantly repeat it. This is a truly unhealthy habit, one that will take us in the opposite direction of happiness.

In these situations, it is also easy to assume the role of martyr and view difficult situations in life as unfair or question why we must face them. This is an extremely unproductive way to think about problems. It solves nothing and leaves us feeling frustrated and sad. Everyone faces difficult situations at some point in life. Most likely, the happiest and most successful people you know and admire have gone through truly hard moments—experiences that shaped them into the incredible people they are today. Success is rarely pure luck; it requires learning, persistence, and courage.

Never forget that you are a meta-thinker. Although any thoughts can cross your mind, you have the power to choose which thoughts are worth keeping and repeating. This means that you can make a conscious choice to face difficulties with a self-determined attitude and interpret any situation in the way you choose. Why not strive to approach adversities with both bravery and positivity?

Yes, you may not always have the power to avoid certain situations in life, but when they happen, you can choose how to react and how much mental space to give them. It is natural to momentarily feel sadness, frustration, regret, or anger. Yet it is important to decide that these feelings will be temporary. You have a choice; it's as simple as making it. Give it a try.

Another important thing to keep in mind when you are facing or moving on from negative moments is that the people who hurt you, whether intentionally or not, are probably not thinking about you. In fact, they likely don't even remember the situation that caused you pain. Why choose to suffer by reliving those experiences?

One of the main reasons it is often hard to let go and forgive is because we let our ego make decisions for us. We hold onto resentment, focusing only on our injured self-esteem. This is unwise. Do not let your ego trap you in bitterness, because resentment is a form of poison. Everyone makes mistakes. Let go and forgive. It will feel liberating.

There is immense power in the words "I'm sorry." Make sure these words come easily to you and offer them when you have done wrong. Accept them graciously when they are offered sincerely to you. Once you make a choice to feel sadness and frustration only briefly, you will be ready to channel your inner warrior.

Your Children Are the Key to Unlocking Your Inner Warrior

You have the power to choose to face problems with a warrior's mindset. When I think of a warrior, I imagine someone who fills me with awe when I see them confront challenges. Warriors fight with admirable courage, passion, and nobility. They are fair, honest, and always defend themselves and those they love. Warriors learn from mistakes and think creatively to find solutions. They are not paralyzed by fear or difficulty. They focus on doing what can be done and don't ponder on the rest. They don't care about others' opinions or judgement. They also know that not every fight is worth engaging in. Warriors turn every situation into a lesson, so they are ready for the next challenge. They choose to see solutions for all problems and help others see and achieve them, too. People will bend over backward to help a warrior because it is absolutely inspiring to witness their courage. Hence, having a warrior's mindset naturally attracts more helping hands.

As supermoms, we have among our incredible powers that of drawing profound perspective and motivation from our children. This includes the ability to channel our inner warriors more easily. Whenever you face a difficult time, think of your children's loving faces and your desire to see them healthy and happy. Let that be the reason to move forward and put on your armor. Focus on their happiness and choose to release the weight of bad moments or the pain caused by others. You can do it. You are a mother. You have endured pregnancies, deliveries, and postpartum challenges; even if you became a mother in other ways, you are still raising children. Who could be braver? Let your children remind you of how brave you are and how brave you need to continue to be for them.

By thinking about your children and how you'd like them to forgive and let go of those who hurt them, you'll find the strength to do the same yourself. This will bring you peace and allow you to model forgiveness for them. Remember, we are constantly teaching our children through our own behaviors. When we choose to forgive, let go gracefully, and face problems with bravery, our children learn to do the same, acquiring valuable emotional tools to face the difficult situations that life inevitably brings. When you face problems like a warrior, learning, forgiving, and moving forward, you become an extraordinary teacher, showing your children how to face life's battles with strength and resilience.

Does This Imply You Will Let Everyone Walk All Over You? Hell No!

In my first job after graduate school, I faced a situation that I did not handle in a way that makes me proud today. I was a rookie, heavily pregnant with my first child. At the time, a colleague openly criticized me for being pregnant, calling women like me "annoying creatures." He did it in front of others and repeatedly suggested that I was solely having a baby to gain more time before my tenure evaluation (a promotion process academics go through a few years after earning a PhD). Instead of responding assertively and speaking up about what I thought about his comments, I mostly stayed silent, intimidated by his seniority. This is one of those moments I wish the more mature and confident version of me could revisit. That's not possible, though, so all I can do is learn and grow from the experience.

I learned a valuable lesson from it—one I want to share with all the mothers reading this book. We should never back down or let anyone diminish us for being mothers under any circumstances. Here is why: Being a mother is incredibly hard, and we do it with immeasurable, selfless love. Our generation will one day age and rely on younger individuals to keep our economy and society alive. Who will fill those roles? Our children and grandchildren. Thanks to our own courage and dedication, humankind survives and transcends history.

So at the very least, we should grow a backbone and enlighten others about this reality whenever they discriminate against, judge, or mistreat women who choose to have children. Standing up for motherhood is just as important when we witness discrimination against other mothers. Never let such behavior go unchallenged in your presence. It is not necessary to create conflict, but we can respectfully educate others about the beauty and strength of motherhood in a constructive way.

The same should be true more broadly if anyone tries to mistreat you or your children. Being forgiving and showing grace does not mean you should stay silent about injustice against yourself or your loved ones. It simply means that after you address the situation, you choose not to dwell on it and then you move forward. When we defend motherhood, we honor those who came before us while facilitating the path for those who will follow.

Tools to Transform into Your Inner Warrior When Needed

My dear Supermom, one of your superpowers is to transform into your courageous and resilient self whenever you choose. Here are a few tools to guide you during challenging times:

1. Realize that you can choose how to face difficulties: Difficulties and challenges will come to your doorstep with certainty. This is part of the human experience. You can only choose how to face them. Do not approach challenges with a victim's or martyr's mindset. Focus on action, learning, and solutions. Be courageous: You've got this; you are a mother—among the bravest and strongest of human beings.

2. Forgive and apologize sincerely to feel at peace and model strength: Let go of resentment by forgiving those who have hurt you, whether intentionally or not. Be equally ready to say, "I'm sorry." We all make mistakes. Offering and seeking forgiveness will not only bring you peace but also teach your children the power of humility and emotional maturity.

3. Draw strength from your children: In tough moments, turn to the love you feel for your children. Let your desire to see them happy and thriving fuel your courage and determination to keep going. Think about how you would want them to face problems, and then, be their example.

4. Stand up for motherhood: When witnessing judgment or discrimination against mothers, speak out with calm strength. Advocate for the power, beauty, and importance of motherhood with pride and grace. We should protect and care for each other.

5. Balance courage with grace: Being kind and forgiving does not mean staying silent in the face of injustice. Speak up with dignity if someone hurts you or treats you unfairly; then let go and move on. Show your children that true strength includes both courage and compassion.

PART III: PUTTING THE FINISHING TOUCHES ON YOUR JOYFUL LIFE

Chapter 7: Gather Wisdom from More Experienced Supermoms

Halfway through writing this book, I had an excellent idea. I realized that a book meant to advise mothers on how to lead meaningful and joyful lives needed to reflect the wisdom from women who have been through this experience. We all can learn from their successes and mistakes. It is not as if we are the first mothers in the world or, for that matter, that I am the only woman who can share her views with other moms. Millions of women have gone through this experience and gathered a great deal of wisdom and lessons. Therefore, I embarked on the mission of interviewing every mother of adult children who I met in the following months.

These conversations were not structured in a formal sense but rather took the form of friendly chats in which I tried to open myself up to other women. I wanted to create a space where they felt comfortable enough to offer a sincere answer to the key question guiding this chapter: "If you could go back to when you first became a mom, what advice would you give yourself?"

Over the course of approximately ten months, taking advantage of the fact that I travel a lot for work, I was able to talk to a couple of hundred mothers of adult children living across the globe. I gathered incredible advice and wisdom from these conversations. I am deeply grateful to all these women for their generosity, sincerity, and kindness.

As different as the conversations were, a handful of topics came up repeatedly. These are the main ideas that I want to share with you in this chapter. Although we have already explored some of these concepts, to further emphasize their importance in your life, I wanted to show you that many of the things we have discussed are also valued by more experienced women.

1. Time with Your Children is One of Your Most Valuable Treasures

A recurrent point in many of the conversations I had was that mothers wished they had enjoyed more of the time they spent with their children while they were growing up. The general advice was to attempt to focus our attention on our children and enjoy the precious, albeit short time we have with them as much as possible.

In the words of a Scottish mom: "I would advise my younger self to reduce my time spent on household chores, or delegate those, if possible, to try to spend more quality time with my children. I spent a lot of time organizing and cleaning, and I know these are good things, but I wish that I had played more with them. They grew up so fast."

The truth is that, as mothers, we are one of our children's favorite people for only a short time. This period is a true treasure. As children grow, they naturally become more interested in others; we have only a small window of time to fully enjoy them while they are still completely ours.

A Swiss mom told me, "It is truly incredible; it almost feels as if you blink, and boom, more than half of your life has passed. When you look back at the end of it all, what stays with you, what brings you the most peace and happiness, are the quality times that you spent with your loved ones, especially your children."

A useful way to be present when we spend time with our children is to consider how temporary each stage of their development is. Each day is precious, and they change quickly, so make a point to create a memory every day and make them feel loved and special. Actively spend time with your children and give them your full attention. Nothing shows unconditional love more clearly than giving someone your complete focus and showing genuine interest in what they like and have to say. Observe your children carefully, try to see things from their perspective, and learn more about their everyday life, their likes, and dislikes. Life is short. What better use of our time could there be?

When spending time with your children, try to choose one or a maximum of two things each day that you would like to guide or correct them on, and resist the temptation to point out everything they do wrong. We need to stop criticizing our children all the time; it is extremely inefficient. When we do, our voices inevitably become background noise. Sometimes it is wiser to just listen and teach our children by modeling through our own behaviors. They will open up more and feel less judged. They will also find their own way. As mothers, we must remember that everyone learns from falling and sometimes our own children will fall. It makes them stronger. Although it might be hard, we need to stop trying to save them from every problem and instead offer our ear, support them through difficulties, and carefully choose a few topics in which to guide them each day. What is most important is to always be there for them with love and support.

2. Set Limits to Take Care of Yourself

Another recurring topic among many mothers that I interviewed was the importance of reminding their younger selves to take better care of themselves. Some of these women were healthy, but others had developed difficult health conditions and now wished they had prioritized their well-being and set firmer boundaries. A woman living in Boston, Massachusetts, told me: "You think you are invincible, that you have unlimited energy and health. However, we are all human. We need exercise, sleep, love, and healthy food. If I could go back, I would tell my younger self to also think about myself, even if just a little bit. Do not get me wrong, I would not change the fact that I was the best mother I could be, but I just wish I had known that I also needed to take care of myself. You see, I am a bit sick today, and if I had only prioritized taking care of my body a bit more, maybe I would feel differently now. Just realize that you will not be young forever, and regardless of your genes, you need to invest in yourself. This way, you will have the strength to care for yourself when you are older."

When I say "set limits," I mean adhering to certain rules that protect your wellbeing while caring for everyone else. These guidelines help keep you happy, healthy, well fed, and balanced in your lifestyle.

How can this be done? Write down everything you ideally need to do each day to be a healthy and whole person. The sky is the limit. Go crazy. List it all on paper or in a file. Think about what brings you joy. What are your hobbies? What activities do you find fun? What things do you truly enjoy but no longer make time for? Then, go over your list. Cross out the items you already do regularly and organize the rest in order of importance. From the remaining items, choose one or two that are most essential to your happiness and well-being. Commit to bringing them back into your life.

My list, for example, includes time spent writing and running—the two activities that keep me functioning at my best for the people around me. They make me happy and are genuinely fun. Together, they take about an hour and a half of my day (thirty-five minutes in the morning for running and fifty-five minutes in the evening for writing). Recently, I made these activities nonnegotiable, setting clear boundaries around them. I initially thought committing my time to these habits would prove impossible and would upset everyone around me, but it turns out that everyone is happier because I am happier. Now I protect this time each day and make sure everyone knows it is not available for anyone else. The rest of my time is fully devoted to my family and my work. Over time, I have learned that protecting this space makes me a more joyful and effective mother and professional.

Choose your actions, the ones that truly count as an investment in yourself. Pick what makes you happy and brings you joy—activities that, when you're older and look back, will make you proud that you took the time for yourself. Then, set firm boundaries to include them in your daily routine.

3. Trust Your Instincts

I had a fascinating conversation with a mother who lived in Costa Rica. She was an accomplished professional (an impressive women, really) with two extremely successful adult children. When I asked her what advice she would give her younger self, she responded, "I would tell myself to trust my instincts. In the end, I have learned that they were almost always correct. Parenting cannot be learned from books; each human being is completely different."

We all need to hear this. It is crucial to remember that we know our children best. We have helped them grow, and because of that, we naturally understand their strengths and weaknesses. Thanks to this deep knowledge and the unconditional love we feel for them, we are often more attuned to the energy that surrounds them and tend to have strong instincts about what might be best for them.

I believe that every human being can perceive the energy of others. Let me give you an example. Years ago, my son was attending a preschool in California where my husband and I met a woman, the parent of one of our son's classmates, whom we jokingly referred to as the "energy vampire." She was someone we both independently perceived as having extremely negative energy. Every time we interacted with her, we ended up feeling upset and uneasy. I cannot explain exactly what it was, but we both felt noticeably drained after speaking with her. What fascinated us most was that we each formed this impression on our own and realized we shared the same feelings only much later.

This is a clear example of the fact that humans can perceive each other's energy and that this perception is valuable. People have both positive and negative moments and react to others and to situations in various ways. We can often read this energy through gestures, posture, tone, words, and overall attitude. Pay attention to how you perceive the energy others project toward you and your loved ones. I understand this ability to sense the intentions or emotional energy of others as intuition. We all have it, and I believe a mother's intuition is especially strong when it comes to her children. This is because mothers pour their love and attention into everything that affects their children. We also happen to know them better than anyone else in the world. As a result, mothers tend to have a heightened instinct about what's best for their children.

Trust that instinct; never doubt yourself. Pay close attention to your intuition. It was built on the incredible legacy of human survival. Your gut often leads you to valuable insights. You can certainly seek advice about your children, but in the end, only you truly know what's best. Listen to your inner voice. When you quiet your mind and stay present, you may begin to receive ideas that seem to appear out of nowhere. Pay attention to them. In my experience, these ideas often relate to problems I am trying to solve, and they frequently offer practical and helpful solutions.

It is incredible what you can achieve when you trust and have confidence in your intuition and decisions. Not only do you feel better, but others can also sense your confidence and are more likely to respond positively. A mother who trusts her instincts and decisions will raise children who are confident in themselves, as well.

4. Life Will Test You—Be Courageous

This point, which we touched on earlier, came up multiple times in my conversations with mothers. Most of them pointed out that it is an inevitable fact that we will face difficult moments throughout our lives. However, many experienced mothers shared that they would advise their younger selves to face tough times with courage. One woman from Italy, a mother of six and now 86 years old, told me, "The one thing that I have learned is that the attitude toward problems ultimately determines how quickly things smooth out or how easily we adapt to new situations. Hard times make us grow the most. These moments are crucial; we need to live them. They are a defining element of who we become. After we face difficulties, we are often changed in profound and better ways; we become tougher and more mature human beings." I think this is one of the most important lessons I received.

As I have pointed out before in this book, I am a firm believer in the power of our thoughts and attitudes to determine the quality and outcomes of our lives. I hope that if you take one lesson from this book, it is this message: You decide the attitude with which you face life, and whether we like it or not, problems and difficulties are often the path to growth.

It is just like learning by doing. Of course, it's not fun to face problems. While we're going through them, such times will test us in unthinkable ways. Yet we will learn a lot from difficulties, and they will transform us into stronger and undoubtedly wiser human beings. Since there's no way to avoid all challenges, when you are faced with one, meet it with courage, maintain a positive attitude, learn from it, and move on.

Another practical piece of advice I received during my conversations with mothers was to be objective during difficult situations. A truly effective way to do this is to try to separate yourself from your emotions in times of stress or when making decisions. Think about the last time a good friend came to you for advice about a tough situation. I'm sure it was easy for you to see a solution. When we assess other people's problems, we are emotionally detached, making it easier to see things clearly and come up with reasonable solutions. However, when we face our own problems, it is often much harder to think rationally or objectively if we let our emotions take over. This is a recipe for disaster. When facing hard times, do your best to set your emotions aside before making decisions. If this feels difficult, it probably means you need more time to reflect, accept, and process the situation. Then, try to approach the problem as if you were advising a friend. Often, when I feel overwhelmed, I ask myself what I would tell a close friend in a similar situation. This exercise always helps me be more objective and separate myself from my feelings.

5. Get Perspective Through Your Children

In our day-to-day routine, we let the nuisances of life get magnified into problems. Many of the "problems" we face are often simply small irritations not worth our time or energy. Yet we sometimes allow them to drain our power and occupy our minds. Of course, everyone faces real and important challenges (as we just discussed), but there are also moments when we sacrifice our peace of mind over things that are not truly significant. These are the kinds of annoyances we will not even remember in a few weeks or months, although they weigh on our minds today.

One incredible antidote to this is thinking about our children. We can look at them, realize that they are a true gift in our lives, and choose to let go of minor nuisances, irrelevant to what really matters. Gossip and ridiculous drama are on this list. What is ridiculous drama? Any issue that you probably won't remember in a year falls into this category. Face it and move on, but please protect your mind from thinking about it. We should not let these nuisances colonize our thoughts for even a second. Instead, we need to train our minds to focus on the truly relevant things in our lives, such as our children's smiles and laughter. When drama rears its head, replace it with the image of your children's smiles, and keep moving forward.

Another good antidote to falling down rabbit holes is to always remind ourselves of our mortality. Life is short. Is it worth spending time on the ridiculous, minor nuisances of life? Absolutely not. No. Stop with the drama. Again, be objective and see each situation for what it is. Separate yourself from your emotions, and try to protect your mental health and frame of mind by minimizing unnecessary drama in your life. Remember, you may not choose the situations you face every day, but you do get to decide how to view them and react to them. Choose to let go of unimportant issues and focus on what matters.

6. Think About Your Future Self

One extremely useful piece of advice came from a trio of mothers—one of them Swiss and the other two American (a Kentuckian and a Coloradan)—who I met in a pool while I was taking a few days off with my family. I wish you could see these ladies. They were the definition of how I want to look like when I am older: fabulous, accomplished, their demeanor screaming "I'm happy and I've loved my life." They told me something important: that one thing they were proud of was that they had invested in themselves consistently throughout their lives, that this was the reason they could afford a fancy vacation and enjoy the luxury of hiking in the mountains at their age. This is crucial. We won't be young forever, and in taking care of everyone else, we sometimes forget to take care of our future selves. We'll need health and money to live well. We'll also need good and sincere friends. Throughout your life, think about your older self and the kind of retirement you want to have. Invest in your physical, financial, and social wealth persistently.

My mom has ingrained this lesson in my mind: save, invest, and think about the life you want to have in the future. I want the kind of life those three ladies were enjoying—healthy, financially independent, blessed with close, genuine friends to travel with. They were also mothers, but that did not prevent them from thinking about their own future.

7. Delegate

Our next bit of advice came from a lady living in Spain. She shared the following piece of wisdom: "There is no way we can do it all well. Happier moms delegate stuff. The more you delegate, the happier and calmer you will feel. If you do not have the financial resources to hire help, then call a friend or family member and ask for a little bit of help occasionally. Also divide responsibilities with your husband or partner, and if your children are old enough, ask them for help, too." I believe this one is extremely important. This is very likely one of the reasons why women could have so many children in the past; they had a lot of support from family, hired help, or community members.

As mothers, we have too many things to do, and we often make the mistake of thinking we are the only ones who can do them well. While we might indeed do things *best*, someone else can usually handle them at an acceptable level. The more help we have, the better we will feel. Delegating not only frees up time to care for ourselves but also allows us to spend quality time with our loved ones.

Try this: List out all the things that you do. Yes, all of them! Now, sit down and really think creatively to identify which tasks can be delegated to hired help or other members of your family. Be willing to sacrifice a little bit of quality (nothing bad will happen), or be open to doing things differently, because this support will open the door to more happiness for you. Go on, do it now. Stop reading and start delegating the things on your list!

8. Stop with the Guilt

How is it possible that we give all we have, our waking thoughts, time, and energy, to our loved ones, and yet we still feel guilty for any little detail that might go wrong or for spending a little bit of time on ourselves? It is as if we have a software for unconditional giving installed in our minds and the minute we deviate or something unexpected happens, we become wracked by guilt. If there is a problem, we feel guilty for doing one thing instead of another. We feel guilty for not being with our children all the time, for their difficulties (which every human inevitably faces), or for taking some "me" time. We sometimes even feel guilty for having professional lives.

Absolutely all the women I interviewed mentioned this point in some minor or major way. Their main advice: Stop. Please stop with the guilt. It is not healthy. It is also unfair to yourself. Of course, you will make mistakes, but you're trying your best. You are human, too. Show yourself compassion.

When guilt starts to show its awful face, look at it head on and tell yourself, "I am an outstanding mother. I wake up every day and try my best to give all I have for my children and my family. I am brave, I have courage, but I also love myself and need to take care of myself to be able to help others. I will not feel guilty about the mistakes I made; I will learn from them. I will not feel guilty for caring for myself, too. I need to do it to be a better mom, to be healthy and happy." Then, in your mind, picture your guilt apologizing for showing up (since you are right) and leaving your mind. Try it out. With time, guilt will show up less in your life.

9. Be Gracious to Your Extended Family

In several of my interviews, we ended up talking about how to navigate relationships with extended families. This was an extremely useful perspective to explore because most of the women I interviewed were mothers and grandmothers themselves. In other words, they were already part of someone else's extended family. As such, they offered incredible insight into this topic.

A Japanese woman married to an American mentioned, "Because we were raised in different households, it is truly likely that we will have different traditions and perhaps opinions from those of our extended families. Almost always, however, our extended families approach us with immense love: love for their children and their grandchildren. They most likely want to do what they deem best in their eyes. So, their comments and advice are always coming from a place of love."

It is important to always try to return that love and have patience because, if we are lucky, we will also be grandmothers or part of the extended family of our children's wives, husbands, or partners one day. Then we will benefit from the same compassion and understanding in return.

10.   Find Your Own Tribe and Seek Their Personalized Advice

Before I finish this chapter, I want to invite you to talk to and seek guidance from mothers you trust, know, and admire. They have more years of experience in motherhood than you and have likely learned a great deal along the way. Yes, times change with technology and cultural trends, but the basics remain the same, and it is very likely that you have a lot to learn from them.

I asked my own mother what she wished she'd known when she first became a mother, and this question led to one of the most remarkable conversations I've ever had with her. I'll always treasure that moment and all the love and wisdom she shared with me. It also helped me realize that many of the worries I have now were also on her mind when she was going through this stage of life. I also spoke with my aunt and my mother-in-law, both extraordinary women, who generously shared their experiences and life lessons with me.

Go and find your own precious tribe, those women you love and admire, and talk to them. Then, ask them the same question: "What advice would your younger self have benefited from upon first becoming a mother? What successes did you have as a mom? What mistakes did you make?" If they know you, they will probably also give you answers tailored to your situation and personality. When you ask another mom for wisdom, especially one who loves you, they are almost always willing to open their hearts to share their most profound lessons to help you. You will learn a lot from these conversations. Listen to them. Really listen to their wisdom. It will help you grow.

Advice from Experienced Supermoms: Things They Wish They'd Known As Young Women

Here is a summary of the main pieces of advice I gathered from our tribe of experienced supermoms:

1. **Time with your children is one of your most valuable treasures:** Be fully present when you are with your children and offer them your complete attention. Few things express unconditional love more clearly than giving someone your full focus and showing genuine interest in what they like and have to say.

2. **Set limits to take care of yourself:** Write down everything you ideally need to do each day to feel healthy and whole. Cross out the things you already do regularly and organize the rest by importance. From the remaining items, choose the actions that feel like an investment in yourself. Pick the things that make you happy and bring you joy; the ones that feel genuinely fun to you and deeply fulfilling. Once you identify them, set firm boundaries to make space for them in your daily routine.

3. **Trust your instincts:** You know your children best. Listen to your intuition: It is rooted in an incredible legacy of human survival and often reveals valuable insights. When you quiet your mind and stay present, you may begin to receive ideas that seem to appear out of nowhere.

Pay attention to them. In my experience, these ideas often relate to problems I'm trying to solve, and they frequently offer practical and helpful solutions.

4. **Life will test you—be courageous:** Difficulties are inevitable. They shape us into stronger and wiser human beings. Since there is no way to avoid all challenges, meet them with courage, maintain a positive attitude, learn from them, and move on. Try to face challenges objectively, just as you would advise a friend. Attempt to disconnect emotionally so that you can think rationally about problems. Only then act.

5. **Get perspective through your children:** Do not allow the little complications of life to be magnified into "problems." Instead, use the gift of your children to gain perspective. They are a true blessing in our lives, and they can help you recognize what matters. Choose to let go of the minor nuisances that are not worth your energy or attention.

6. **Think about your future self:** Save, invest in both your physical and financial well-being, and make choices based on the kind of life you want to have in the future.

7. **Delegate:** List all the things you do. Identify which tasks can be delegated to hired help or other members of your family. Be willing to sacrifice a little bit of control or perfection. Be open to doing things differently, because accepting support can open the door to more happiness and freedom in your life.

8.   Stop with the guilt: When guilt starts to show its awful face, tell yourself, "I am an outstanding mother. I wake up every day and try my best to give all I have to my children and my family. I am brave, I have courage, and I also love myself. I need to take care of myself to be able to care for others. I will not feel guilty about the mistakes I made; I will learn from them. I will not feel guilty for caring for myself, too. I need to do it to be a better mom, to be healthy and happy."

9.   Be gracious to your extended family: Their actions often come from a place of love. Be patient because, if we are lucky, we'll also be grandmothers or the extended family of our children's wives, husbands, or partners one day. When that time comes, we will hope to receive the same compassion and understanding in return.

10.   Find your own tribe and seek their personalized advice: Go and find your precious tribe, those women you love and admire, and talk to them. Then ask them: What would they advise their younger selves when they first became mothers? What successes did they have? What mistakes did they make? If they know you well, they will probably also give you answers tailored to your situation and personality.

Chapter 8: Let Your Mortality Inspire You to Live a Present Life

If we reflect on what we know about the length of life on this planet or the universe's time scale, each of our human lives is remarkably short. The latest research suggests Earth is approximately 4.54 billion years old, while the average life expectancy of women, who on average live longer than men, is about 80 years. If we were to scale Earth's age to one year, the average woman's lifespan would be just 0.55 seconds, and the history of all human civilization would last only 69 seconds of that year.

These numbers are a reminder that all human lives are finite, and whether we like it or not, one thing is certain: We will all die someday. All our relationships and life phases are temporary. Yet we tend to forget just how precious and short our time is. Most of us, on an average day, spend most of our waking hours on autopilot, moving from one activity to the next, and rarely feel fully present or recognize that each instant we breathe is precious and finite. In fact, the present moment is the only thing we really have.

How can we leverage our mortality to be more present? I firmly believe that keeping in our minds the certainty of our mortality and the temporary nature of all things can be a useful tool for appreciating each moment of our lives, being more present, and investing our time wisely. Below are some suggestions that can help you savor your precious time on this beautiful Earth.

Be Conscious of the Temporary Nature of All Things

Sahil Bloom makes an excellent argument about the scarcity of time and its consequences for the meaning of our closest relationships in his book *The 5 Types of Wealth: A Transformative Guide to Design Your Dream Life*. He effectively argues that we share only a short part of our lives with our loved ones. For example, we are only our children's favorite person until they are about ten years old. After that, they will probably prefer their friends and boyfriends or girlfriends. Moreover, they will get busier and busier, with ever less time to spend with their parents. In other words, all that surrounds us today, including our most precious relationships, will likely shift or change in nature over time. Hence, we truly need to enjoy these times and create more opportunities to be fully present with our loved ones, especially our beautiful children and our aging parents, because these relationships are also transient and will transform into something new. This will help us savor and enjoy our time with them even more.

Let your Mortality Motivate You to Move Out of Your Comfort Zone

Dearest Supermom, you are remarkably brave. Honestly, being a mother is not for the faint of heart. You are guiding and molding the life of another human being and giving it your all in the process to see them shine. This is probably one of the biggest, most difficult, and incidentally most rewarding life purposes. Likewise, you expect and attempt to teach your child to take risks in life, push out of their comfort zone, and care absolutely nothing for the judgment of others. You probably tell your children, as I tell mine: "Your life is limited. Make the best of it. Do not be afraid to try new things and take risks. It is a bad investment of your time to spend even one second contemplating others' opinions on your life choices." You need to take the same advice to heart.

You have only limited time. Let your mortality be your greatest motivator to lead a great life full of courage and adventures. Your mortality should give you the courage to stop being afraid and push yourself out of your comfort zone, to act and achieve your highest goals. Never spend even two seconds worrying about what others think of you. People will always talk, and they will always have an opinion, but at the end of the day when you die, who cares? What did it matter?

I will tell you what will matter: that you had fun, challenged yourself, and tried with all your being to go after your goals and build your unique and authentic joyful life. If you give your best effort, there will be no regrets. You will also learn and grow in the process.

In short, let your mortality inspire you to be your authentic self, unapologetically. Your time is limited. Be bold. Be brave. Follow your heart.

Embrace Nature to Savor Your Finite Time

Regularly immersing ourselves in nature can enhance our appreciation for life's finite moments. It is a great investment of our time and helps us feel happier and replenish our energy. Extensive research has shown that time in nature dramatically improves our mental and physical health for multiple reasons. It grounds us and helps keep our thoughts in the present, increasing our mindfulness. Visually, nature has a calming effect that reduces anxiety and stress, and the sounds of nature are extremely soothing for the mind. Additionally, there is better air quality in nature, and receiving sun each day boosts vitamin D, both of which have positive effects on physical health. Even a few minutes during the week around your house or in a nearby local park can work wonders for your energy, happiness, and sense of fulfillment.

An alternative that was successful for me was to begin with five to ten minutes outdoors each day. I now spend that time running in the mornings. Try to begin only with the amount of time you feel you can credibly commit to while you create the habit. You'll start to see that once you're outside, you feel better, and you'll begin to crave that time every day. Potential outdoor activities include gardening, sitting in the sun, practicing any outdoor sport, sitting in a green area with friends, going for a walk in a leafy neighborhood, walking your dog, and my personal favorite: spending time with your children outdoors. This last one is special because you are taking care of yourself while also contributing to your children's well-being. If it is difficult for you to spend a few minutes in nature every day, perhaps because you live in a busy city with limited options, another alternative is to spend longer periods of time in nature during the weekend.

Our family especially enjoys hiking together on Saturday or Sunday mornings. We have one rule on these hikes: No technology, except to take pictures of something exciting. Our beautiful two-year-old goldendoodle gets euphoric when we take him hiking—almost the same reaction he shows when we travel and return after a few days away from him. He runs fast from side to side until he is exhausted. Then he recovers and does it again and again. It makes me smile just thinking about it. I imagine this might be how our body and mind feel after we spend some time in nature. My children also love this time and get excited about the adventure; they are also calmer and happier afterward. My husband and I have also discussed how lovely this time is and how well we feel afterward.

Another beautiful exercise I'd love for you to try outside is to pause and truly marvel at how perfect, complex, and stunningly beautiful nature is. Do not take it for granted. Make an intentional effort to fully appreciate the magnificent experiences you get to enjoy while in nature.

Each tree, each flower, each creek, each season, and each animal hold its own kind of magic.

Marveling at nature and feeling grateful for the absolute privilege of experiencing it can be an incredibly grounding and fulfilling practice. I don't know how we have forgotten just how astoundingly beautiful and perfect nature is, but we must not take these everyday miracles for granted. That cannot be. It would be an extremely sad existence. Try to rediscover and marvel at nature every chance you get. Nature should certainly be on the list of things to be grateful for every single day.

If you absolutely cannot carve out time in nature on certain days, you can still bring it into your life through nature sounds in your playlists or visual images in your physical spaces. Plenty of research shows that these sights and sounds are also soothing and grounding for the human mind.

Our Mortality Is a Motivator to Be Present and Find Beauty in the Ordinary

If you are like most people, you probably spend considerable time wishing and dreaming you were somewhere else, in some past or future. We are almost never fully in the present, and we spend even less time enjoying ourselves. There is almost always something we are waiting to achieve, something we wish to have, or some moment we long to share with others. Our inner monologue meanders like this: "When I have a better job, or when I have more money, or when I am on vacation, or next Friday, I'll be content." But if we spend most of our time thinking about another time, we will blink, and our lives will already be in the past, only for us to realize we enjoyed our time on this earth very little.

All in all, what I want you to internalize is that human lives are short. Really, really short. This is not a dramatic statement or something to be depressed about. It is just the factual truth. This fact of our existence should motivate us to be present and, most importantly, attempt to enjoy our present time. It may be difficult to be fully present absolutely all the time, but try to enjoy your day-to-day, approach each day with a good attitude, and find joy in the little things that add up to make a life.

Also try your best to enjoy the journey of everything that you do. There is always another task, another objective, a new milestone—but what will matter at the end is that you enjoyed the journey. Realize that, in fact, the majority of your life is spent on different journeys and by savoring them you'll be savoring your life.

Tools to Leverage the Certainty That Our Lives Are Finite to Live a Present Life

Below you can find a summary of some actions you can take to have a more present and peaceful life:

1. Be conscious of the temporary nature of all things: All that surrounds us today will likely shift or change in nature over time. Create opportunities to be fully present with your loved ones because these relationships are also transforming us into something new.

2. Let your mortality motivate you to move out of your comfort zone: Your mortality should give you the courage to stop being afraid and push yourself out of your comfort zone to act and achieve your highest goals. Never spend even two seconds worrying about what others think of you. If you put in your best effort, there will be no regrets. You will also learn and grow in the process.

3. Embrace nature to savor your finite time: Potential outdoor activities include gardening, sitting in the sun, practicing any outdoor sport, sitting in a green area with friends, going for a walk in a leafy neighborhood, walking your dog, and my personal favorite: spending time with your children outdoors. Try to clear your thoughts in nature by concentrating on what you feel and marvel at the incredible miracles around you. Attempt to begin with 5 to 10 minutes; if that's not possible, then try to do it during the weekends. You can still bring nature into your life through nature sounds on your playlists or visual images in your physical spaces.

4. Our mortality is a motivator to be present and find beauty in the ordinary: Human life is short. Try to enjoy the day-to-day, approach each day with a good attitude, and find joy in the little things that add up to make a life. Let little dramas pass you by without affecting your mood— they're not worth it!

Chapter 9: Continue Growing and Learning

Your children's goals and dreams are not your own. I know that some of you may not like this statement, but it is true. First, your children are entitled to their own dreams and goals. While you can guide them, celebrate their achievements, and cheer them on, they are independent human beings with their own opinions and preferences. Second, you are also entitled to have dreams and goals beyond being a wonderful supermom. For many of us, one of our greatest dreams in life has been to become mothers, not just any mothers, but outstanding ones who want to watch their children thrive and find happiness. While this is deeply meaningful and true for most mothers, it does not mean that we cannot pursue other dreams and goals, as well. Nor does it mean that our children's dreams and goals are automatically our own. We are all independent humans. While we support our children with all our energy, we are also free to nurture our own aspirations.

Every human being needs continuous transformation and growth to thrive. Cultivating new dreams and goals is an essential part of any mother's holistic well-being. I dare you to reflect on your life and consider what your goals are, besides continuing to be an outstanding mother and enjoying that process. For many of you, this might be extremely clear, but maybe you're not sure what your goals are. Setting goals is a dynamic process, and goals can change at any time; you only need to make up your mind about whatever they are. They can be incredibly ambitious, or they can be simple. They can take any color or form. What matters is that they are yours, what makes you tick and smile with emotion.

Design Your Perfect Day

A good practice that helped me clarify my current life goals is to reflect on what my perfect day would look like. I first heard of this practice in Martha Beck's interviews. It involves finding a quiet space where you can relax and, without filters, think about your most perfect day. You must do this without second-guessing yourself or questioning where your mind goes. Visualization is extremely powerful, so it is important that you imagine it in as much detail as possible. Think about what you see and what you feel with your senses. Everyone's perfect day will be different. It does not need to be glamorous, colorful, or expensive. It can be whatever your mind wants it to be—the only important part is that it is uniquely yours.

Let me share a glimpse of my own perfect day: I open my eyes without any alarm. I feel rested and happy. I am in my house, where we live right now. I hear birds and my children playing and talking together downstairs. I look out the window and see beautiful green trees, lots of flowers, and a sunny day with fantastic weather, not cold but not warm either. I look to the other side of the bed and see my husband sleeping soundly, handsome and healthy. I kiss him and stand up to look at myself in the mirror. I look healthy, rested, happy, and beautiful. I go to the bathroom to take care of business and head downstairs. My kids are happy to see me, and my dog goes crazy happy (as he always does) when I wake up. I cook a delicious and healthy breakfast surrounded by music (breakfast is my favorite meal of the day). We get ready, and I drop off the kids at school. Then I head upstairs to my home office, my sanctuary, to spend some hours writing and working on my research. My office is exactly as it is today, in front of a gorgeous window where I can see many trees and roofs. I relax my mind and start typing. I think of all the people I want to help and draw inspiration to write for them. I write to create value for them.

After a few hours, I go running with my dog through a neighborhood full of colorful flowers. When we get back, I take a wonderfully relaxing bath, and then it is lunchtime. I make my lunch while video chatting with my parents and siblings. The menu: avocado toast with cappuccino. I eat outside in my front yard while talking with them in the sunshine. Then it is time for more writing, more research, and then *more* coffee (the juice of the gods!). I head to my local coffee shop, where I spend a few more hours writing. I absolutely love working in coffee shops. I write and write, and then it is time to pick up my kids. Back home, we find my husband there, too. We all spend a fun afternoon making art, playing soccer, reading, dancing, and eating delicious food. Then we put the kids to bed and spend some quality time together before going to sleep ourselves.

That's it! My perfect day. At least it's my perfect day today, what I want to be doing right now. It was beautiful for me to realize this because I understood that I'm a researcher and writer at heart and that, for now, I want to keep doing this work every day. It also made me realize that I love running, spending time in my garden, drinking cappuccinos (although everyone who knows me knows that!), and being with my family. Seeing this day clearly in my mind motivated me to write this book. It helped me realize my true reason and purpose in writing academic papers and books: to inspire positive change in the world. We all have tough moments, and we all can use some guidance. I'd love to inspire you to try this exercise and find your own goals and dreams, to identify your own life purpose, your own perfect day.

I share such a private part of myself with you to dare you to dream for yourself. Others' judgment of my perfect day is irrelevant; likewise, I expect you to care nothing for others' opinions of yours. Your perfect day is yours to have and yours to share if you wish.

The more often you do this exercise and the more detail and emotion you pour into your visualization, the more effective it will be. This is because you first need to conceive your perfect day in your mind to act and make it a reality. Everything that exists in the real world was first conceived in someone's mind. You need to see where you are going to make it happen.

Dare to Go for It

Once you have gone through this exercise, you'll know what your goals are. Next, you need to believe in yourself, be brave, take risks, and start acting. You'll be able to achieve anything you want if you align your positive thoughts with your actions. I dare you to have your own dreams and goals, be brave, and take action to achieve them. Identify your goals, have faith in yourself, and act. Act, act, and act. Wake up every morning and visualize these goals. The more you do it, the clearer and easier it will be to align your actions with them. Just begin, little by little, action by action, and you will get there.

So go and be happy, my dear Supermom. Continue being a supermom—just be a *whole* supermom. One unafraid to care for herself, get out of her comfort zone, spend time with her friends and loved ones, invest in herself, and pursue her dreams, all while wearing her heart on her sleeve for her family. You absolutely deserve it.

More Information

For additional content and tools for supermoms, please visit:
www.super-mom.net

or follow the book's Instagram account:
supermom.lovelife

For more information about the author's professional work, please visit:
www.sandrarozo.net

www.ingramcontent.com/pod-product-compliance
Lightning Source LLC
Chambersburg PA
CBHW051631120626
46551CB00014B/2028